Discovering
STAINED GLASS

John Harries

Revised by Martin Harrison,
Curator of the Stained Glass Museum

Shire Publications Ltd

CONTENTS

Cover photograph: St Thomas at St Mark's, Friday Bridge, Cambridgeshire, designed by Robert Turnill Bayne, 1866, and made by Heaton, Butler and Bayne.

ACKNOWLEDGEMENTS

Photographs are acknowledged as follows: Hallam Ashley, plates 7–10; Martin Harrison, plates 11–15, 17, 18 and cover; Victoria and Albert Museum, plates 1–6, 16.

Printed in Great Britain by C. I. Thomas & Sons (Haverfordwest) Ltd, Press Buildings, Merlins Bridge, Haverfordwest.

THE STATE OF STAINED GLASS TODAY

Nearly every church or historical building that we enter has some stained glass. Sometimes, it is true, it is broken and patched, and the window space has to be made up with plain modern glass. But the great cathedrals and famous abbeys and churches that have become places of cultural pilgrimage seem to have plenty of it. And even modest churches that we visit in passing are more often than not full of brightly coloured scenes in stained glass. These facts, especially the latter, give the impression that an ample amount of rich stained glass has come down to us from distant times, and in fairly good condition. But this impression is a false one. Compared to the wall paintings that once decorated medieval churches, a great deal of early stained glass has survived—certainly enough to make it a rich field of interest. But a far greater amount has been lost to us.

A pair of field-glasses is almost essential to the enjoyment of detail and drawing in windows, as they are often high and inaccessible. Focus the field-glasses on a small roundel, or a face in a medieval window, and compare the standard of draughtsmanship with that of a nineteenth century window. The difference is clear and exhilarating. Looking at a nineteenth century window which seems so assured and complete, one is not prepared for this revelation that the art can be raised to so much higher a pitch. Even a fragment of old glass, if it is well preserved, has so much more to offer. This brings us to the second reason why we are not as rich in stained glass as we appear to be. That is that very often windows six or seven hundred years old have not been well preserved.

The Damage Done through Ignorance and Neglect

Glass and lead are durable substances, but they do not last for ever. They are fairly frequently subjected in this country to high winds and to rain. There will come a time when the leads weaken, and the cement which makes joints watertight begins to leak. Then damage will be done to the inside of the glass. And on the outside the glass is gradually eroded by the rain, until it becomes coated with a white chalky layer. In this way the glass loses its clarity and is eventually reduced to a crumbling mass. Any painting on the outside of the glass is effaced. The iron bars used to support the window on the inside can be weakened by rust, and the cement which fixes them in the stonework can crumble away. When this happens the stained glass windows hold the bars in place, not the other way round, and this imposes additional strain on the leads.

At this stage a window is due for preservation, and here two things can go wrong—the preservation may be done badly, or it may not be done at all. This latter is undoubtedly the reason why such vast quantities of good stained glass have simply disappeared. The glass in its weakened state may have been blown in by the wind. It may have been knocked out to make way for something new, and supposedly better —or at least cheaper than the cost of restoration. Or it may even have been allowed to drop out.

The eighteenth and nineteenth centuries are partly to blame. One may read an account of the seventeenth century which suggests that the glass is in a reasonably flourishing condition. A visitor in the next century finds it weakened, broken, and much reduced in extent. And a visitor in the nineteenth century finds that it has gone. Sometimes it has been moved to another church, or the broken odds and ends used to fill up a window in the same church. But this comes under the heading of restoration not dilapidation.

Restoration

Here, too, the whole business has been managed much too haphazardly. Incumbents have not been sufficiently interested or efficient, perhaps regarding the stained glass as the province of the cleaners and builders. The result is that leading has been entrusted to the local plumber or ordinary glazier, not to stained glass artists. So, thick leads were used that destroyed the fine drawing and outline of the windows. Faces can be seen in windows with a thick band of lead running across them, or with a network of such leads, giving them an odd and clumsy appearance. This was the common way of mending cracks, and it is the wrong way. A reinforcing sheet of plain glass should be used, and held in place with double-thick leads.

Sometimes windows which had been taken out for cleaning and restoration were replaced inside out. In this way delicate painting which had been kept safe for centuries was exposed to the elements. Much restoration work consisted of replacing a piece of broken or eroded glass, or of repainting a piece which had become worn. Such painting was often done by hacks, and when this is so the crudeness is obvious. Even when it has been skilfully done there is usually a detectable difference. For it has proved impossible to recapture the spirit in which the early stained glass artists worked, and with it, the way they painted hands, faces, or clothing—faces especially.

Very little of the stained glass we see today has escaped

some restoration. If it has been done fairly skilfully, or only in a few places, we can still enjoy the window. We may not even notice it, or only on close inspection and comparison through a pair of field-glasses. Many pictures in galleries have been retouched, or repainted in surprisingly large areas, and we do not think a great deal worse of them for that. But what of those windows where a light, or window opening, has been made up of assorted panels or figures, roundels and shields, bits and pieces of borders and patternwork by the same artist—even by different artists, or from different churches? After all, one would not dream of grafting a head from one picture by Leonardo da Vinci on to a figure from another—let alone adding a background from Raphael, and a supporting cast by Pollaiuolo. The result would be interesting, but ridiculous. And yet a surprisingly large number of windows are like this, though perhaps not to such an extreme extent. They are often still enjoyable. The overall design has been sacrificed, but rich colour and beautiful drawing of detail may remain. It says much for the robustness of stained glass as a medium that it can be mutilated in this way and still retain some of its beauty.

There was one other practice quite common in the nineteenth century. That was the removal of an original window, and the substitution of a carefully aged fake. This was not necessarily done with criminal intentions. Though in many ways given to self-doubt, the nineteenth century artist was in others remarkably confident. More often than not the firms entrusted with the restoration probably felt they were supplying a superior article, and simply stored the original glass. But sometimes they did dispose of the glass illegally and at a profit, by selling it to a private collector. In fact this is another reason why some stained glass is not available to the public. There was nothing to prevent owners of manors or churches from selling glass, if they were hard up. No doubt, though, the amount that has disappeared in this way is not great.

The position now is slightly better. For some reason people are now more aware of the fragile beauty of historical places in general. They visit stately homes and cathedrals in unparalleled numbers. Programmes on television, and books help to inform people and awaken an appreciation of things such as stained glass. This general atmosphere is fighting the ignorance that has allowed stained glass to become so dilapidated in the past. All new designs for stained glass windows have to be approved by Diocesan Advisory Committees. Quite a few churches where a pride is taken in the stained glass are now kept locked. Whatever this says for the rôle of the Church, it protects it from vandalism. It is usually possible to get in by going to the Rectory, or other place indicated on the door, and asking for the key—not always, however.

Nevertheless, while all this is encouraging, still not enough is done to preserve our great inheritance of stained glass. In this sphere, Diocesan Committees are not empowered to act —they can only give advice. All this is an anomaly. Good paintings of the past are preserved as if they were the product of a greater creative genius than stained glass. Whereas in fact the best stained glass windows were probably made by men who in a different age would have been outstanding painters.

Damage Done from Religious Motives

At various stages in history stained glass windows have been destroyed for religious reasons. In the middle ages men throughout Europe had one religion—Catholicism. There is a deep connection between stained glass and Catholicism. Both of them originate from southern Europe and the Near East, and neither could flourish indefinitely in the colder soil of northern Europe. Stained glass is ritualistic, emblematic, highly coloured, and mysterious, and so was Catholicism. Stained glass coloured the facts of life, and transformed them into something intense and strange.

On the one hand both stained glass and Catholicism were aware of the enjoyment and fulness of life, of its colour and appeal to the senses. And on the other there is at the heart of both a kind of yearning for something simpler and more mystical. One can see this in the faces of figures in early glass, surrounded as they are by all the richness of their trappings and background. They seem preoccupied, bent always upon something more spiritual. This leads to a curious tension within the art and within the religion.

Slightly paradoxically, therefore, stained glass tends to be at variance with any faith that insists simply upon the life of the spirit, and attaches little importance to the arts. Such a faith was that of the Cistercian Order, and they are the first people on record, not as destroying stained glass, but as trying to prevent its spread. In 1134 they were told that they could use only white glass in their churches, without any figures or "crosses" in it. The influence of this in Britain was probably slight. In the first place stained glass had been longer established on the continent, and the Cistercian ordinance would have a correspondingly larger impact on it. And in the second place, even there it could have made only a small impression on churches outside the Order. Writers have often exaggerated the effects of the ordinance, claiming that it was responsible for the kind of window known as *grisaille*.

The term comes from the French word "grisailler", meaning "to paint grey". Grisaille windows consisted basically of white glass, decorated with patterns in a grey oxidised paint, occasionally enlivened by a touch of colour. The patterns were taken mainly from the shapes of leaves. These windows therefore satisfied the requirements of the Cistercian ordinance. But their widespread use must have had other causes. These probably included a wish for more light, and a shortage of skilled stained glass artists. The main cause, however, was expense. In the twelfth century, windows were increasing in size and number, and had to be filled somehow. If a donor could be found, they could always be replaced by something more elaborate later on.

Stained glass is also at variance with any outlook that insists upon the plain or prosaic qualities of life, and distrusts the exotic and entertaining. This is where the history of destruction really does come in. For when, in the sixteenth century, Protestantism began to assert itself in the northern temperament, and the Reformation ousted Catholicism from Britain, stained glass was outlawed. It was not only a religious matter, it was a struggle for power. But whatever the motives, a royal Injunction of 1547 states:

> "*Also*, that they shall take away, utterly extinct and destroy all shrines, coverings of shrines, all tables, candlesticks, trindles or rolls of wax, figures, paintings, and all other monuments of feigned miracles, pilgrimages, idolatry, and superstition; so that there remain no memory of the same in walls, glass-windows, or elsewhere within their churches or houses. And they shall exhort all their parishioners to do the like within their several houses."

The old faith was to be discredited, and all traces of it wiped out.

Many churches did follow these instructions, and replaced the stained glass with white. At St. Michael-at-Plea it was planned to spend twenty pounds on "the new glassing of xvij wyndows wherein were conteyned the lyves of certen prophane histories, and other olde wyndows in our church". At St. Lawrence's church in Reading the operation cost £15. 10s.6d. Carrying out the Injunction was an expensive business. But it could be carried out without replacing the windows—simply by knocking them out. At Long Melford in Suffolk, "Fyrmyer the Glasyer of Sudburye" was paid eleven shillings "for defacing of the sentences and imagerie in the glasse wyndowes".

This meant that the furniture and materials inside the church would suffer, and the church would be unusable in winter if the windows were not covered in some way. The Royal Injunctions of 1559, one year after Elizabeth's accession, closed up this loophole, by adding to that of 1547 the words: "preserving nevertheless or repairing the walls and glass windows". Stained glass windows were elevated to the status of "Monuments of Antiquity", especially if commemorative of a donor, and it became an offence punishable by prison to "breake downe or deface any image in glasse-windowes in any Church, without consent of the Ordinary".

Amid all this official confusion, what really happened during this period? The answer is that after being condemned and then reprieved, stained glass was finally allowed to waste away. It is given us by William Harrison, rector of Radwinter in Essex, in his *Description of England*, published in 1577:

"As for churches themselves, belles and times of morning and evening praier remain as in time past, saving that all images, shrines, tabernacles, rood loftes and monuments of idolatrie are removed, taken down and defaced: Onlie the stories in glasse windowes excepted, which, for want of sufficient store of new stuffe, and by reason of extreame charge that should grow by the alteration of the same into white panes throughout the realme, are not altogether abolished in most places at once, but by little and little suffered to decaie that white glass may be set up in their roomes."

The main reason for the change in policy is clearly stated: expense.

But the forces opposed to Catholicism and stained glass did not really concentrate themselves until the coming of Cromwell and the Commonwealth in the next century. "Superstitious pictures, images, ornaments, and relics of idolatry" were anathema to Cromwell, and in 1640 their destruction was ordered. This was confirmed by the House of Commons three years later, and there began the greatest deliberate onslaught on stained glass in its history.

The fanatical William Dowsing, who held the office of Parliamentary Visitor from 1643, gives details in his diary of a journey through parts of East Anglia, undertaken for the express purpose of stripping the churches of ornament and smashing the stained glass "like a Bedlam". Glass in several of the great cathedrals was destroyed by Cromwell's soldiery: "Lord, what work was here! What clattering of glasses! What beating down of walls! What tearing up of monuments!" Stained glass was associated with "damnable pride" and "the father of Darkness". Richard Culmer, the rector of Chartham —"Blue Dick"—broke as much glass as possible at Canterbury Cathedral. He came to the "Royal" window, and climbed to "the top of the citie ladder, near 60 steps high, with a whole pike in his hand ratling down proud Becket's glassy bones". It was quite common at this time to remove or break only the heads of figures—even of the dragons in tracery lights in one instance. Sometimes, as in East Anglia, faces were merely scratched across. Where these windows have survived, this has been one of the causes of restoration.

But, extensive as this destruction was, it would be wrong to blame it for the disappearance of the greater part of stained glass. The accounts of Dowsing himself, and of the antiquaries of the seventeenth century, especially the royalist Richard Symonds, make it plain that a great deal of glass remained, though often in a poor state of repair. This tallies with William Harrison's story of gradual "decaie". And stained glass making had not stood still since the Reformation. Even if the figures of saints were banned, it was all right to decorate windows with floral designs, or with heraldic shields. In fact this period saw a great rise in the popularity of heraldic subjects. The objection was to religious pictures, not to stained glass in itself.

Stained glass, then, has had its ups and downs in official favour, but its constant enemy has been neglect—neglect, and the gradual erosion of time.

THE STATE OF STAINED GLASS IN THE
MIDDLE AGES

A Medieval Church

If we now have an incomplete impression of the former glories of stained glass, what was a medieval church like when in its prime? It was very different from the rather sombre affair of today. Colour was everywhere. Pillars and arches were painted and walls were adorned with murals. The woodwork of screens, doors and roofs was carved and gilded. Among all this shone window after window of stained glass, depicting the central themes of Christianity.

We often have a total misconception of the medieval church and the state of mind that inspired it. That state of mind was not one of peace and the tranquility one associates with grey stone walls. These are qualities that time has imparted to our churches. The state of mind was instead one of dramatisation, of ambition and ferment. It aspired to be nearer God, and yet could not escape the turmoil of the everyday world. Death and physical hardship were familiar figures: they harrassed men in the plagues, and battles, and in a way of life that was often brutal and unyielding. The presence of physical pain made the delights of physical pleasure all the more dear. And so they celebrated the joys of this world, and of religion, and feared the life to come.

The Two Purposes of Stained Glass

Under these circumstances, stained glass windows were more than just decoration. This is often how they are regarded today, and it is a mistake. To the clergymen who had them put in churches, they had two uses, over and above making their churches more beautiful. They taught the fundamental facts and lessons of Christianity to the people, and they helped to move them with its spirit, to awaken in them a sense of devotion.

While the church played an accepted part in the lives of ordinary men, going to church must have retained an element of strangeness for them. Church services were in Latin or French, languages that most of them could not understand. There were no books to help them—very few people could read anyway. They were surrounded by the mysteries of the priest and his intonation, and the unfamiliar splendour of the building, its symbols and decoration. Many must have found this combination bewildering: some would be lulled by this, infused with a sense of things beyond the ritual ; others would be merely bored by it. For both kinds there were only two

10

ways to penetrate through the mystical aspects of the service to plain guidance about Christ's life and its meaning for them—and those were the sermon, and the stained glass windows or wall paintings.

Often, no doubt, the priest would point out the meaning of the windows, in the same way that he would elaborate on texts from the Bible. Stained glass windows have often been called "the Bible of the poor". In this way laymen could gain a knowledge of the life of Christ and his saints, the miracles they performed, the teachings of the Old and New Testaments, and of what would happen to them when they died. The sources and subjects of the windows are discussed more fully in a later section.

But what must have been the effect on an uneducated man when he looked up at a stained glass window! Surely not just one of a lesson learned. Remember that he had to look up—this was something higher than himself. And what he saw was the light, which he knew as daylight, and knew to be white, being resolved into a thousand colours and tones, as brilliant and intense as any jewel. This fact alone must have struck some of them as a wonder. They were not sophisticated, besieged with colour on all sides as we are. These were virtually the only pictures they saw, and they were pictures in light, that most intangible yet basic of all things.

It has been suggested that this is what gives stained glass its mysterious devotional power. Light was to the medieval mind the source of all life, a power for good poured on to the world from the fountainhead of heaven. And stained glass converted this into something he could see, and see a meaning in. It changed light into something that made sense in terms of everyday life. This change was probably associated in some obscure way with the idea that "the spirit became flesh", and that this was the way in which it played an active part in life.

I say "obscure" because people would not, of course, look at stained glass windows with this metaphysical theory in mind. Nevertheless it does go some way towards explaining the devotional function of stained glass in the medieval church.

The Spirit of the Age

It is not fanciful to see in the stained glass and other decoration of a medieval church a deep and serious religious purpose. The windows of the period impress us by the single-mindedness which they bring to the quest for faith, or to its celebration.

This may surprise us when it is considered that the crafts-

11

men who made the windows were, after all, ordinary men, not saints and visionaries. But there is no real contradiction here. For the skill which made the windows belonged to the individual, but the conviction that what they depicted was true belonged to all. Given skill and sensitivity, a man would be able to draw the face and figure of Christ at the last supper with solemnity and majesty. This was not because he had cultivated an insight ignored by other people—as would be the case today. The opposite was true. He could achieve this, with the utmost simplicity, just because he knew what all men knew.

It can justifiably be said therefore, that churches were built and decorated "to the greater glory of God". This does not mean that people did not sometimes have selfish motives in making donations. Nor does it mean that craftsmen worked for a penny less than they could get, or that their heads were always full of noble and reverent thoughts. It was simply that no man could do otherwise than bear witness to what were acknowledged to be the facts of Christ's life and mastery.

It was the spirit of the age, and because it was a simple and literate spirit, it will not come again. No amount of ingenuity can recapture it—only parody it. This is why the Victorian revival of the medieval in stained glass was bound to fail.

The Medieval Stained Glass Craftsman

The earliest window-makers were known by the Latin word for a glazier *vitrarius*. By the twelfth century this had changed to "verarius" or "verrarius". It is hard to say exactly what was meant by this title, but it can be taken to imply the making of stained, as well as white, glass. It would have been difficult to make a living solely out of the production of white glass windows.

It is often assumed that these men were monks, but it has been seen that this was not the case. In the early days at least, the monasteries dedicated themselves entirely to worship. Worldly pursuits, including arts such as stained glass, were shunned. By the fifteenth century, the monasteries had fallen away from these high ideals, but even so, stained glass windows were still supplied by laymen.

They would receive a thorough grounding in the art as an apprentice in a workshop, their progress being supervised by the "master glazier". Owing to the prominence of France in this field, stained glass artists in the thirteenth century were often called "verrers" or "verrours", from *verre*, the French word for glass. In the fourteenth century, when we were more

12

independent of French workers, these terms gave way to "glass wryghte" or "glasenwright", which was derived from the old English word "wyrhta", meaning a worker. By the end of the century this had again been replaced by the titles "glasier" or "glasyer". These continued until the seventeenth century when "glass painter" came into use. As will be shown in a later section glass painting was in fact a different process from what we know as glass staining, and one that only developed in the sixteenth century. "Glass stainer" was first used in the eighteenth century.

Comparatively large numbers of people were employed in the making of stained glass. About 45 names are known in the period up to 1300, more than 75 in the fourteenth century, and over 70 in the fifteenth and sixteenth centuries—and there must have been many more. There were great centres of manufacture at York, London, Oxford, Canterbury, and other cathedral cities.

Some of these people were no doubt jobbing craftsmen who supplied simple stained glass at a cheap rate. But the master glaziers of the larger firms were important people, as well as being brilliant craftsmen. They were honoured by civic posts. The portrait of Thomas Glazier of Oxford was even included in a window of Winchester College—a privilege usually reserved for the donor of the window. The major stained glass artists were on good personal terms with what we should now call the establishment.

They formed themselves together into guilds, to regulate matters of work, and to protect their interests—against foreign competition, for example. This proved necessary, because from about 1490 onwards both Henry VII and Henry VIII encouraged foreign craftsmen to live and work in this country.

As early as the thirteenth century there was an office known as King's Glazier, which by the fifteenth century carried with it an allowance of a shilling a day. The duties were to glaze and repair windows in any building belonging to the king, or founded by him—though the holder could also take on outside work if he wished.

The medieval stained glass maker was above all, then, a lay craftsman. Whatever the nobility of the windows he created, he himself needed careful watching. This explains the length of many contracts, and the heavy stress laid on using the best materials and new designs, with the most conscientious methods.

The Price of Windows

Similarly the medieval craftsmen knew exactly what his work was worth, and made sure he got it. There was thus considerable variation in the cost of windows, and in their quality. The cost was worked out at so much the square foot. In the fourteenth century we read of 13d. a square foot being paid for windows in Windsor Castle, and in the fifteenth of figures such as 1s., while by the sixteenth century the price for good quality work had risen to 1s. 4d. or 1s. 6d. a square foot. But the price was variable, and cheaper glass could be obtained. The highest recorded price, however, was 2s. a square foot. This was paid to John Prudde, who was appointed King's Glazier about 1440, for windows executed for Warwick Church in 1447. As a contract could run into a thousand square feet or so of glass, and money was worth very much more then, furnishing a church with stained glass was evidently an expensive business.

Changes in the Craftsman's Attitude

But in spite of the money involved, the first consideration of the craftsmen of the twelfth to fourteenth centuries, was the presentation of the canons of Christian faith. This was the spirit in which work was commissioned, and craftsmen remained true to it. The early craftsmen, therefore, had a simple and unpretentious style.

But as time went on, the nature of the craftsmen changed. By the end of the fifteenth century they were concerned with the elaboration of their work. The prime object of the windows almost became lost amid the proliferation of detail. They were more worried about the niceties of their work than about its meaning. Whenever this happens in an art, decadence sets in and so it was in the time of the Renaissance in the sixteenth century. The results are sometimes exquisite, but always weaker than in early glass. The seventeenth and eighteenth centuries brought further changes. Enamel paints became popular, and artists set out to imitate the realistic effects of oil painting. The soul, which had already begun to slip away from stained glass in the sixteenth century, disappeared entirely.

THE SUBJECT MATTER OF
STAINED GLASS WINDOWS

Something has already been said about subject matter and its purpose. But the stained glass artists of the middle ages drew on far more sources than have yet been indicated. Only a small proportion of these would find their way into the ordinary parish church. In the larger churches, however, the range is very wide indeed.

Most of the incidents depicted took place in the holy lands of the middle east, centuries before they were commemorated in stained glass. The men who made these windows were therefore at a disadvantage. Travel was not common then and they knew little of the clothes and architecture of the time of Christ.

So they showed things as they knew them. Dress, armour, ships, interiors, and buildings are all medieval. This may have had the effect of making the lessons of the windows more relevant to people. At any rate, it was unavoidable.

Figure Windows

Pictures of **Saints** were very popular. There were almost four thousand saints to choose from, including many that we hardly remember. They are usually shown holding an emblem, and their names are often written in Latin, particularly from the fourteenth century onwards—"Egidius" for Giles, "Jacobus" for James, "Hieronymus" for Jerome, and so on.

Many of them were patron saints or protectors, and so were shown several times in the same church. St. Christopher was particularly popular, because anyone who looked at his picture was supposed to be safe from sudden death on that day. Various saints were believed to be able to protect suppliants against disease or misfortune—St. Lucy against eye diseases ; St. Roch against the plague ; and St. Apollonia against toothache. It was this kind of belief that was later denounced as "superstition". Others were patron saints—St. Nicholas of children, sailors, thieves, and pawnbrokers ; and St. Catherine of schools and learning.

The clothes worn by these figures were rich, formal vestments, not everyday wear. Deep blue was often substituted for the black worn by Benedictine saints such as St. Maurus, as it was not easy to reproduce black in stained glass.

These figures of saints are not to be confused with windows telling the **Stories of Saints' Lives,** their miracles and martyrdoms. These were ambitious subjects, and are usually found in larger churches. The windows were based on the account of the lives of the saints in *Legenda Aurea,* the *Golden Legend.* This was a popular book in the middle ages, compiled in the thirteenth century by a friar who later became Archbishop of Genoa. It was originally in Latin, but it was published in English by Caxton in 1483. Its author had called it simply *Legends of the Saints,* but it came to be called the *Golden Legend* because of people's respect for it. This was not the only record of the saints' lives used as a source. There were also the *Dialogue of Miracles,* and the *Mirror of History,* both thirteenth century productions.

15

These really belong to the class known as "picture windows". But there were other kinds of figure window. The **Nine Orders of Angels** were often shown, especially in traceries. They fall into three groups and were depicted in a great variety of ways. The first group consisted of Seraphim, Cherubim, and Thrones, all supporting and worshipping God's throne. The second was the Governors of the Universe—Dominations, Virtues, and Powers. The third group was Principalities, Archangels, and Angels—the Messengers of God's Will.

The **Twelve Apostles** and **Twelve Prophets** were also used to make series of figure windows. By tradition the Apostles were supposed to have contributed one clause each to the Creed which became the canon of the Catholic religion. So each figure is shown holding an emblem, and also a scroll on which is written his article of the Creed. Thus St. Peter stands with his keys of gold and silver, and the text: *Credo in Deum Patrem Omnipotentem creatorem coeli et terrae*— "I believe in God the Almighty Father, Creator of heaven and earth". There is an intact medieval series at Fairford in Gloucestershire, and a complete seventeenth century series at Wadham College and Lincoln College, Oxford. Many churches have incomplete series.

The Twelve Prophets were designed as a parallel to the series of Apostles. They were never named or given emblems, but they, too, carry scrolls, this time with a quotation from the Old Testament. Obadiah, for example, carries the inscription: *Et erit regnum Domini, Amen.*—"And the Kingdom shall be the Lord's. Amen". Once again, there is a perfect series at Fairford.

Picture Windows

A popular source of inspiration for these was the illustrated Bibles such as the *Mirror of Man's Salvation* and the *Biblia Pauperum* or *Bible of the Poor*. These were reproduced in manuscript by laymen. They followed the pattern of contrasting one or two pictures from the Old Testament with one from the New. The pictures from the Old Testament are called "Type", those from the New, "Anti-Type".

Type and Anti-Type, together with a text, made up a commentary on the life of Christ. The same pictorial scheme was followed in windows. The best-known example is in the twelfth century "Theological" windows of Canterbury Cathedral, and there is a sixteenth century example at King's College, Cambridge. Occasionally, too, windows were derived from the work of a popular religious writer—such as the sixteenth century *Pricke of Conscience*, by Richard Rolle.

1. Westminster Abbey, Jerusalem Chapel. Thirteenth century.

2. Canterbury Cathedral, window in south transept. Methuselah. Twelfth century.

3. Wells Cathedral, Lady Chapel. Angel from a doom. Fourteenth century.

4. New College, Oxford. Angel.
Late fourteenth century.

5. Victoria and Albert Museum,
London. Angel playing a rebeck.
Fifteenth century.

6. Victoria and Albert Museum, London. Head of a monk. Fifteenth century.

7. St Andrew's, Norwich. Dance of Death.

8. St Peter Mancroft, Norwich, east window. Bible stories. Fifteenth century.

9. At the works of Messrs G. King and Son Ltd, Norwich. Applying trace colour to glass for a window for St Thomas's church, Norwich.

10. Leading a window at King's Norwich Works. This is part of the fourteenth-century Jesse window of Cartmel Priory.

11. Stained Glass Museum, Ely Cathedral. Detail of the Last Supper by William Price the Elder (1702), formerly part of the east window of Merton College chapel, Oxford.

12 (opposite). St Alkmund's, Shrewsbury. The Assumption of the Virgin, by Francis Eginton, 1795 (after Guido Reni).

GLORY OF GOD. IN MEMORY OF THE REV JAMES COLVILL... THIS WINDOW IS OFFERED BY HIS... A.D. 18...

14. St Mary's, Mortlake, London. *The Annunciation*, by Henry Holiday, 1866.

13 (opposite). St Martin's, Worcester. *Transfiguration* designed by Frederick Preedy, 1857.

15. Stained Glass Museum, Ely Cathedral. The Agony in the Garden of Gethsemane by Heaton, Butler and Bayne, 1866, formerly in St Andrew's, Bridport, Dorset.

How great rejoicing was made for the wedding of St. George and the Princess

16. Victoria and Albert Museum, London. Scene from St George and the Dragon. Designed by D. G. Rossetti and made by William Morris in 1862.

17. Misterton, Nottinghamshire. The Five Wounds, designed by John Piper, 1966.

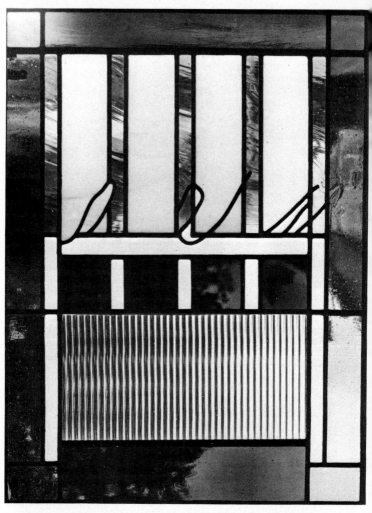

18. *A window in a private house at Birchover, Derbyshire, designed by Brian Clarke, 1977.*

The **Old Testament** provided many stories suitable for picture windows. Common ones, especially in the fourteenth and fifteenth centuries were the Creation, the Deluge, the story of Adam and Eve, and histories of Abraham, Jacob, Joseph, Moses and Aaron. These were often made into a series. There is an outstanding example of such a series at Great Malvern Priory in Worcestershire, where 33 panels remain from the original 72. Other series or part-series remain at Barkway (Herts); Thaxted (Essex); St. Neot (Cornwall); Hereford Cathedral; and Lincoln Minster.

New Testament windows were usually based on the **Life of Christ.** The window-makers would often lead up to this by illustrating the birth and upbringing of Mary.

They would start with the story of Joachim and Anne, the grandparents of Christ. These stories of Christ's background would be taken from the apocryphal gospels of the second century, which after centuries of rejection, had now come to be part of the Catholic tradition. Incidentally, the medieval bible which furnished these subjects was not the Authorised Version of today. It was the Vulgate edition, so called from the Latin word *vulgata,* meaning "popular". This was a fourth century translation into Latin of the Hebrew Old Testament and the Greek New Testament. It is still the authorised version of the Roman Catholic Church.

The type of window known as the **Tree of Jesse** was very prominent. This, too, had to do with the antecedents of Christ, showing his descent from Jesse, the father of David. The window was literally a picture of a family tree. Jesse was positioned at the base of the window, and from him rose a vine which spread right across the window, ignoring the stone frames. The decorated stem twisted into ovals, and each one contained the splendid figure of one of Jesse's descendants. Kings were nearest the trunk, and the prophets who told of Christ's coming were nearest the outside. At the top of the tree were Mary and the infant Christ. There are good fourteenth century examples at St. Mary's Church, Shrewsbury, and Wells Cathedral—and fifteenth century ones at Margaretting (Essex) and Leverington (Cambridge).

A window would often be filled with panels depicting the **Seven Sacraments.** These were: Baptism; Confirmation; Marriage; Penance; Holy Orders; Holy Communion; and Last Rites. They were arranged round the figure of Christ crucified or risen, each sacrament receiving a stream of blood from his wounds. There are imperfect examples at Crudwell (Wilts.); Doddiscombsleigh (Devon); Buckland (Glos.); Combs (Suffolk); Great Malvern Priory (Worcs.); Melbury Bubb (Dorset); and Tattershall Church (Lincs.).

There were also the **Seven Works of Mercy**—Feeding the Hungry, Giving Drink to the Thirsty, Clothing the Naked, Housing the Stranger, Visiting the Sick, Visiting Prisoners, and Burying the Dead. These can be seen at Chinnor (Oxon.), Combs (Suffolk), and Tattershall (Lincs.)—and a seventeenth century enamel-painted series can be seen at Messing, (Essex).

There is an unusual window at St. Andrew's Church, Norwich. It shows the Dance of Death which was a common scene in medieval art. Death leads all kinds of men off to his kingdom in a macabre dance—a subject which would have been suggested by the Black Death of 1348-50.

Apart from windows showing the Seven Deadly Sins and Te Deum, which remain only in fragmentary condition, the only kind left to consider is the **Last Judgement or Doom Window.**

The vision behind this was on a grand scale, and the subject was given an important position—usually in the large east or west window. Sometimes, however, it occurred in the tracery lights of Jesse windows. This is the case in Wells Cathedral and Winchester College chapel.

These windows gave great scope for the artist's invention, but always followed the same general layout. The lower part of the window is given over to the souls who, having risen from their graves, are being judged by St. Michael. Some pass St. Peter and enter heaven. Most are dragged off to the torments of hell, which are shown vividly. Kings, popes, and bishops are often among the damned—no soul was saved simply by virtue of his office, only by being good.

Above all this rises Christ in majesty, flanked by the Virgin Mary and St. John. The Apostles might also be included, and traceries were often filled by angels summoning the dead. There are well-known examples at Fairford (Glos.), Ticehurst (Sussex), and Tewkesbury Abbey.

A detailed knowledge of sources is not important in enjoying stained glass. But it does help to remove some confusion if types of windows can be identified by the viewer. And this alone tends to increase the pleasure gained.

THE TECHNIQUES OF STAINED GLASS

Historical Origins

The first people to make glass systematically were the Egyptians. In about 300 B.C. they invented the blowpipe—a tube four or five feet long used to blow the soft, heated glass into a bubble, so as to thin it before shaping it and cutting it into sheets. The method will be described in more detail later on. The blowpipe is the instrument still used in making fine quality glass.

This glass would be nearly opaque, and accidentally coloured by traces of metallic oxides or salts. Glass was rare. It could be almost as valuable as jewels, and the Egyptians sometimes used it in a similar way—for ornaments. They also, however, used it for filling very small windows. The Phoenician traders brought glass and a knowledge of glass-making to Greece and Rome. Slabs of window glass have been found at Herculaneum and Pompeii, and also in this country at Silchester. The Romans cut round windows in walls, and set the glass in frames—the forerunners of the armatures used in medieval glass.

It was not until the early Christian period that a way of making transparent glass — called "crystal" glass — was discovered.

Thereafter, we find various mentions of glass and window-making. In 410 St. Jerome and St. Chrysostom record the existence of glass windows. And in 680—the earliest mention of glass in this country—Benedict Biscop, Abbot of Wearmouth, sent to France for glaziers to work in the new churches at Jarrow and Wearmouth. (Glass excavated here is on show at Jarrow Hall Museum.) In 709 St. Wilfrid had the windows of York Minster glazed. This was not the York Minster we see today, but its predecessor.

In these early windows, glass was used as an alternative to oiled cloth or paper, or small sheets of horn. But what kind of glass was it? The most likely answer is that it was a sort of mosaic of plain glass, relieved by bits of coloured glass, probably still obtained accidentally. There are fragments of this on the continent and presumably English glass followed the same pattern.

And then, in the year 1065, we find stained glass windows as we know them at Augsburg Cathedral. In 1066 the first Benedictine monastery at Monte Cassino was provided with stained glass. The stained glass at Le Mans dates from about 1090, that at St. Denys, Paris, and the cathedral at Chartres from the middle of the twelfth century.

Obviously then, stained glass developed rapidly on the continent during the hundred years after 1066, the time of the Norman conquest of Britain. But in Britain, during this period, there is no mention of stained glass.

And then, about 1145, we have a Tree of Jesse window at York Minster. There is a remarkable resemblance between figures from this and ones at Chartres and St. Denys. They must have come from the same basic pattern. Chartres was a great centre for stained glass in the twelfth century and workmen must already have come over. Certainly there was a fresh influx in 1170, when they came to glaze the great new cathedrals built by the Normans.

Stained glass as we know it had arrived. And it had arrived suddenly and apparently fully-fledged as an art. As early as 1020, indeed, a monk called Theophilus had compiled a book called *A Study of Various Arts,* in which the technique of making a stained glass window was set out in full—a technique that remains largely the same today.

This might lead us to suppose that there were in existence prior to the Augsburg Windows, large numbers of windows, which have completely disappeared. But this is extremely unlikely. It is true that the Augsburg windows are the products of a highly developed technique, and have a tradition behind them. But that tradition was probably that of enamelling, not of complicated glass-work. Stained glass is very like enamel work in technique, especially the kind of enamel called "cloisonné". This name comes from the French word for a partition. "cloison". The idea is that areas of enamel, are separated by partitions of metal strip, which go to make up the lines in the design. These resemble the leads of stained glass, and enamel is a coloured glassy substance made in a similar way to stained glass.

The technique of cloisonné work originated in Byzantium, later known as Constantinople, in the eighth century, and had reached France by way of Venice by 972. And apart from the glass makers already in Europe, a colony of Venetians settled at Limoges in France in 959. Limoges was later to become a great centre for enamel work. These glass-makers, too, derived their skill ultimately from Byzantium. What probably happened, then, was that the glass-makers pooled their knowledge with the enamellers to produce glass and designs of the type seen at Augsburg.

Both of them were working in the Byzantine tradition. This involves the kind of art we associate with icons and mosaics —sometimes static and calm, sometimes full of movement, but always richly decorative, holy, and ritualistic. It was this tradition that laid the foundations of the Gothic style in Europe. This is the influence that we first see at work at Augsburg, and which was later introduced to this country.

How Glass Was Made

White glass was made from sand, soda or lime, and potash, by mixing them and melting them in a clay pot in a furnace. The last two ingredients acted as flux to assist the melting process. The potash was obtained from the ash of plants. At white heat the materials fused and formed liquid glass, which was allowed to cool until it could be picked up on a blow-pipe. It was called "metal".

It was coloured by adding various metal oxides to the mixture before melting. Copper oxide produced red, or ruby ; cobalt oxide produced blue; manganese oxide gave purple glass ; and iron oxide made various greens or a bright yellow according to the amount and temperature used. Impurities in these oxides led to a very wide range of colours.

The furnace used at this stage was made of clay or brick, shaped like a dome. It had three layers. The first contained the log or charcoal fire. The second contained the pots of glass, and the third was used for forming the materials into a kind of slag, ready for use in the pots.

Glass which was coloured right through was known as "pot-metal". There were two ways of making the soft, heated mass of glass into the sheets required for windows. One was called the cylinder or "muff" process and the other the "crown".

In the muff process, a lump of the metal was collected on the end of the blowpipe, and blown out like a balloon. At the same time it was swung to and fro by the glass-maker, so that the balloon became elongated. But it was a slow process, and the glass might have to be re-heated at the "glory hole" or opening of the furnace. When the balloon of glass was the right size and length, it was detached from the blowpipe, and opened out at both ends with a caliper-like tool. It was then cylindrical in shape, and looked like a muff. The muff was split along its length with a hot iron, and softened again in a furnace. It only remained then to flatten it out with a wooden tool. Sheets so formed were probably small—about 12in. by 10in.—and were called "tables".

In the crown process the blowpipe was rolled back and forth and the spinning, hollow ball of glass was gradually opened out with the caliper tool. The balloon-shaped glass was gradually transformed to a circular sheet, or crown, and when this was completely flat, it was broken off the blowpipe. It was thickest in the centre, and between 12in. and 24in. in diameter.

Sheets of glass were annealed for one to four days. It can be seen therefore that making enough glass for a large window would require a great deal of time, care, and patience. Whether crown or muff glass has been used in a window can be told from the direction of the minute air bubbles in the glass. In muff glass they form straight, parallel lines, while in crown they form widening concentric circles.

There was another kind of coloured glass, apart from pot-metal. This was called "flash" glass. It was made by coating or "flashing" white glass with a thin layer of coloured glass. Flash was thus more transparent than pot-metal—an advantage with the dense ruby colour. Later flash glass was also produced in blue and green, but these were not much used. It was made by collecting coloured glass on the blowpipe first, and blowing it out into a small bubble. This was then dipped into white glass several times, until a large mass had been gathered. This was blown into a large balloon, which was treated in the usual way. As a result the white glass was coated on one side with the coloured glass. Later it was discovered that rich patterns could be obtained by scratching away parts of the thin layer of coloured glass. This was known as "abrading".

One other colouring method, sometimes used in conjunction with abrading, needs to be mentioned, and this is "staining". In this process, discovered in the early fourteenth century, glass was painted with a preparation containing silver sulphide or chloride. When fused in an oven, the silver produced a yellow colour. Subsequent stainings and firings could produce a deep orange. This innovation was important because it enabled yellow and white shapes to be shown on the same piece of glass. Previously, when the artist wished to show a yellow crown, halo, or hair, on a white head, he had to cut out and fasten two separate pieces of pot-metal —yellow and white. Now all he had to do was paint the crown, and draw the face, on one large piece of white glass. This was easier and cheaper. It led to a refinement of drawing that some welcome, and others deplore as weakening the essential character of stained glass.

Details of faces, folds of clothes, and background patterns were all drawn in with a special dark paint, which was then "fixed" by firing. The pigment was copper or iron oxide, and soft powdered glass was mixed with it to work as a flux. The medium which enabled it to be spread on the glass was wine or urine.

The Price of Glass in the Middle Ages

The only glass made in England, until the sixteenth century, was white glass. The chief centre was at Chiddingfold in Surrey. Glass was sold by the "wey" or "ponder", a "ponder" being 5lb. In the fourteenth century a ponder could cost from 6d. to 9d. Coloured glass was imported from the continent. There were two main places of manufacture — the Rhine Valley and Normandy. Glass from the Rhine was called "Reynyshe" or "Rheynish", and was shipped to such ports as Hull. Glass from Normandy, on the other hand usually entered this country through a southern port. The tendency was for English window makers in the south to use the greenish glass of Normandy, and in the north to use the clearer glass of Germany. Norman glass in the fourteenth century could cost 6d. a square foot, and coloured 1s., while German coloured glass could cost from 2s. 2d. to 3s. 7½d. a ponder, depending on colour. At this stage blue glass seems to have been the most expensive.

As the centuries passed, glass became thinner, clearer, and smoother. This was not an improvement. The rough texture and consistency of earlier glass were in themselves attractive, and when they went, much of the richness of stained glass went with them.

How Stained Glass Windows Were Made

The first step was to measure the windows to be filled, and to take "templates" or copies of their shape. A trestle table was then coated with whitewash. On this was drawn the design. Charcoal was used for outlines, flesh areas were painted red, and the lines cf the leads were boldly painted with a brush. Later on the cartoon, as it is called, was sometimes drawn on parchment. This enabled designs to be traced, and it was easy to obtain a variety of designs simply by making a few changes in the course of tracing.

The job of drawing the design on the table was the responsibility of the master glazier, or principal of the firm. At Westminster, in 1351, such men were paid 1s. a day. Often the person paying for the window left its design to the discretion of the master glazier, but sometimes detailed instructions were given.

When the cartoon was ready, pieces of different coloured glass were placed over it, before being cut to shape. They were given their rough shape by being split with a hot iron. Water was used to start the crack. The pieces of glass were then trimmed with an iron tool called a "grozing-iron" or "groisour". This was not unlike the back of a modern wheel glass cutter, and was used to snap small pieces from the edge of the glass. The men who did this job were paid 6d. a day. Diamond cutters were not used until the seventeenth century.

The glass was put in position over the design, and details of the face, drapery and lettering painted in. At first all this was done purely in line, but later on washes were used to show shadow. The paint used was the dark, all-purpose one already mentioned. The brushes used were made from many different animal hairs—among them being hog, squirrel, badger, cat and marten. The men who did the drawing ranked next to master glaziers, and were paid 7d. a day. The best of them could draw with brilliance and freedom, and did not copy the lines of the cartoon too exactly.

Silver staining was also done at this stage. The glass was then fired in a kiln different from the furnace used in its manufacture. The construction of the kiln or muffle was simple. Several sticks were bent into the shape of arches, and their ends dug into the ground. This framework was covered with a mixture of clay, dung, and hay, the layer being about four inches thick. Iron bars were pushed through the tunnel so formed from one side to the other. These supported the iron tray on which glass was placed for firing. A layer of whitening was sprinkled on the tray before the glass was put on to it. A hole was left at the top of the kiln.

When the glass had finished its firing over a white hot fire of beech logs, it was sealed in the kiln and left to cool.

The cool pieces of glass were laid out again on the table, and fastened with the leads. These are grooved strips of lead roughly H-shaped in cross-section. They were made in two ways. In the first a wide, flat box was filled with reeds laid side by side. Molten lead was poured in, and when it had cooled, the reeds were slit along their length, and pulled out of the thin lead strips so formed, leaving a groove along each side. These strips were called "calmes" from the Latin for reed — *calamus*. In the second way, the grooves were simply scraped out of strips of lead. Nowadays lead is milled—a method which started in the seventeenth century.

While the glass was being joined with these leads, it was held in place with nails. These were called "closing" or "clorying" nails. When the panel had been built up it was surrounded by an extra thick strip of lead. If the window was a rectangular one, a wooden frame could be used to hold the glass steady, in addition to the nails. The leads were soldered at each joint, wax, fat or resin being used as a flux. The window was turned over and soldered on the other side. A waterproof cement was rubbed into the gaps between leads and glass to protect the window.

Every opening in a window is called a light. If this was large, it would need several panels to fill it, and these would have to be supported. The greatest danger was that of being blown in by wind, so the support had to be on the inside. For this purpose vertical iron bars, called "stanchions" or "standards", were set up, crossed by horizontal ones, which were known as "saddle-bars" or "sondlets". The window was tied to these by strips of lead soldered to the leads.

This, however, was a later method of fixing windows in their openings. In the twelfth and thirteenth centuries windows were sometimes held in place by iron armatures whose shape was tailored to that of the panels. The panels were fixed to the armatures with eyelets and wedges, and the armatures were held fast in an oak frame which ran right round the window opening. This system can be seen at Canterbury.

THE HISTORICAL DEVELOPMENT OF STAINED GLASS

The Twelfth Century, or Byzantine Period

There were five types of window in this period: Pattern Windows; Figure Windows; Medallion Windows; Jesse Windows; and Rose Windows. Window openings were large and single, and had the round Norman top.

Only a minute proportion of twelfth century glass remains. Most of it is at Canterbury Cathedral. Much of it has been moved from where it was placed in 1184. There are smaller amounts of twelfth century English glass at Dorchester Abbey (Oxon.), Brabourne Church (Kent), and York Minster. For comparison, there are also some panels of twelfth century French glass at Rivenhall Church (Essex), and Wilton Church, near Salisbury.

The only existing twelfth century example of a **Pattern Window** is at Brabourne. It is a simple geometrical design based on semicircles and petal shapes. These are formed entirely by the leads—there is no drawing on the glass. It is a mosaic of clear though greenish glass, relieved only by touches of colour. It is the forerunner of the grisaille glass already described, and is the simplest possible advance on plain white glazing.

There is a superb series of **Figure Windows** at Canterbury, showing the Ancestry of Christ. Thirty eight remain from the original eighty four, and are now in the south transept and nave. The usual position for figure windows at this time was in the clerestory. Each light contains two figures with names inscribed, set one above the other. They are seated on thrones, and surmounted by simple arches or canopies.

The figures have an alertness, dignity, and simplicity of drawing that places them among the great achievements of stained glass. This remains true in spite of the fact that hands and feet have often been badly restored, and borders have often been removed. These borders ran right round the window frame and were 7 or 8 inches wide. From the beautiful examples in medallion windows in the Trinity Chapel at Canterbury, we can tell that their absence from the figure windows is a great loss. They are finely drawn, and of unparalleled richness of colour and design.

Again, the best twelfth century **Medallion Windows** are at Canterbury, in the north choir aisle. They show Old and New Testament subjects from the *Biblia Pauperum*. There are also medallion windows at Dorchester Abbey, based on the life of St. Birinus.

It will be gathered from this that medallion windows show incidents and groups of figures. They are set in circular or square frames, a number of such medallions going to make up a window. Each one was surrounded by a thin border of patterned glass, or strapwork as it is called. The background to the medallions was decorated with formalised leaf-patterns, the colours counterchanging with those of the medallions. The whole was surrounded by a wide border of the type described. The medallions were built up like a mosaic, in strong, intense colours—mainly ruby and blue. Often as many as 100 different pieces of pot-metal would be used in a medallion only one foot across. The drawing was in line only, and brushwork was sensitive and vigorous. In the Canterbury glass the eyes of figures are opened wide, and the pupil is shown as a large black dot. This gives the faces the peculiar compelling quality of an icon. Haloes at this stage are always shown by a separate piece of glass. The setting of an incident is shown in a symbolic, stylised way: there is no attempt at realism. Outdoor scenes are represented by a tree or building, indoor ones by arches. Artists at this time were not concerned with creating the illusions of scale and perspective. What we have instead are magnificent, jewel-like pictures.

What was happening in the medallion was explained by a latin script. An area of glass was covered with the dark paint used for drawing, and the letters were scratched out of this with a sharp stick. The kind of lettering used here is called "Lombardic", which is far easier to read than the "black letter" or "gothic" script which took its place about 1375.

There is no complete twelfth century example of a **Tree of Jesse Window,** but a panel remains at York. Jesse windows were evidently far less elaborate than in the fourteenth century, consisting of only a few figures.

Rose Windows were the great round windows in cathedrals, the stone mullions within them often suggesting petal-shapes. The only twelfth century example of the stained glass used to fill them is at Canterbury, though it is incomplete. The subject is the Old Law, and the window originally showed Moses, the Cardinal Virtues, and Great and Minor Prophets —an ambitious scheme.

The Thirteenth Century, or Early Gothic Period

The rounded Norman windows gradually gave way to

single pointed ones. These are called lancets. Later in the century two or more might be placed side by side. A new kind of window makes its appearance—a combination called **Medallion and Grisaille.**

The black oxide paint commonly used for drawing was now applied to **Pattern or Grisaille Windows.** Designs were often based on leaves, which showed a tendency to become increasingly realistic, though still stylised. Often, too, the background was cross-hatched. Another type of grisaille window consisted of complicated geometrical patterns of interlaced strapwork heightened by colour. The lozenge shape was important in most grisaille glass. The borders of windows were much thinner than in the twelfth century, and the patterns less varied. Increasingly-natural foliage often alternated with pieces of plain coloured glass. In this century the leaf-patterns were confined within each pane of glass. Later they were so arranged as to suggest that they were covering the glass, as tendrils wind round a trellis. There is one exception to this— the five huge windows at York Minster called the "Five Sisters", which foreshadow the development of grisaille glass in the next century.

Only fragments of **Figure Windows** remain from the thirteenth century. They are gathered in the north, south, and east choir aisles at Lincoln Cathedral. They closely resemble the figure windows of the twelfth century.

Medallion Windows differed little in design from twelfth century examples. There was, however, slightly more emphasis on detailed drawing. Beautiful patterns were used in backgrounds. These are called diaper patterns, and were obtained by scratching through a matt of the dark oxide paint. The borders right round the windows were thinner, and starting to become less inventive in design. New subjects were added, such as the Lives of the Saints. There is a wonderful series of windows showing various miracles in the Trinity Chapel at Canterbury.

Towards the end of the century, artists started letting small panels into grisaille glass, thus giving rise to the **Medallion and Grisaille Window.** The shape of the medallions varied— they could be circles, oblongs with trefoil heads, quatrefoils, or pointed ovals. These windows were at once cheaper and more luminous than medallion windows, and more interesting than plain grisaille ones.

The medallions often contained single figures—saints, or apostles, for example—and there are hints of a pose very characteristic of fourteenth century work. In this, the figure is gracefully, almost languidly, draped in an S shape. These medallions are simpler than earlier ones, and made of larger pieces of glass. This can be seen especially in the drapery, which has fewer folds. The flesh colour was much lighter, and hair was drawn on the same piece of glass as the face, though haloes were still separate. Foliage grisaille was more popular as a background than the strapwork kind.

An important variation, which appeared about 1270, was the heraldic window. The brightly coloured shields were the pointed, curved sort, and contained only one coat of arms. They were usually placed at the bottom of the window.

Parts of **Tree of Jesse Windows** survive at Salisbury Cathedral, Lincoln Minster, and Westwell (Kent). From them, it can be seen that the curves of drapery, figures, and vines had become more flowing. At this time, the tree filled only one lancet, or at the most two. The colour of the ovals containing the figures was often counterchanged with that of the background panels, the usual contrast being blue and ruby.

The only remaining thirteenth century **Rose Windows** are the "Dean's Eye" and the "Bishop's Eye" at Lincoln Minster. The Dean's Eye is the more complete, though patched in places with other thirteenth century glass. It is 24 feet across, and shows the Last Judgement.

The Fourteenth Century, Middle Gothic, or Decorated Period

Windows were larger now, and divided into two or more lights. These had trefoil or cinquefoil heads, surmounted by tracery lights. Between the lights ran stone mullions. These changes eventually resulted in the Perpendicular style of window. The geometrical iron armatures of the twelfth and thirteenth centuries gave way to saddle-bars.

Silver stain was introduced, with the consequences already noted. As the century progressed, the colour and texture of the glass lost some of its richness. Yellow and green grew in popularity at the expense of blue and ruby. White glass became clearer, and tended to replace the pink-brown glass previously used for flesh. Coloured glass was often decorated with scratched diaper patterns. These were based on foliage and show great imagination. A pattern resembling seaweed was popular. The S pose for figures became increasingly prominent, and leaves or plants were more realistically drawn. Another thing which creates a strong difference in style from the previous two centuries is the placing of a fairly complicated canopy above figures. This century also saw the rise of heraldry as a subject for windows. Stained glass became more "decorative". About 1375 the change to black-letter script took place, and latin is often used for dedications. Scs

(Sanctus) denotes a male saint, S̄ca (Sancta) a female one. Pph or ppha shows a prophet.

In **Grisaille Windows** cross-hatched backgrounds disappeared, and the leaf shapes became recognisable as vine, ivy, hawthorn or oak, and so on. They were no longer restricted to individual shapes of glass, but were allowed to grow in sprays over the whole window. Silver stain was used to enrich these leaf designs, and further interest was added by small shields or roundels, or emblems such as the keys of St. Peter, or a pelican. The pelican was shown wounding herself so that her young could drink her blood. This was a popular medieval legend. There are some particularly attractive shields at Tewkesbury Abbey and Gloucester Cathedral.

Involved strapwork designs were succeded by simpler arrangements of "quarries" (French *carreau*). These were lozenge—or diamond-shaped pieces of glass. But as usual at this time, the foliage drawn on them spread over the whole window.

Figure or Subject and Canopy Windows are the most typical windows of the period. The figure was set under a canopy resembling those in ancient tombs and brasses. Canopies became more and more complicated, and in the end occupied much of the upper part of the window. Sometimes they had birds perched on them, or were topped by fantastic turrets of German inspiration. At first architectural details in the canopies were scraped out of black paint, but later silver-stained white glass became popular. At the end of the century figures stood on bases such as tiled pavements.

The coloured figure-and-canopy panels were generally placed half way up the lights, the rest of the windows being filled with grisaille, set off by a shield or roundel. The panels thus made a band of colour separating two white bands. Sometimes a simple group of figures based on Biblical subjects was shown under a canopy, instead of a single figure. Backgrounds were often coloured and diapered. Borders were now narrow, and made up of motifs such as fleur-de-lis, or oak-sprigs, alternating with blocks of red or blue glass. This kind of border was comparatively mechanical, but still attractive.

Saints are often shown with their emblems. In many cases the hair is drawn with a beautiful rhythmic flow. The general use of pattern in the best decorative work is extraordinarily assured and satisfying. Smeared shading is occasionally used for faces, but as yet the modelling is tentative. From this time onwards the figure of the donor is often shown, kneeling in prayer at the foot of the window.

The kind of window showing **Panels and Single Figures on Grisaille** was a direct development from the medallion and grisaille window of the thirteenth century. Treatment of the medallions was the same as for figure and canopy panels. The Virgin and Child was an especially popular subject in addition to the usual scriptural ones. Alternatively, single figures were put straight on to a decorated quarry background. This was rare in the fourteenth century, but was to become a favourite style in the fifteenth and sixteenth centuries—for the figures of donors, for example.

There are some fine examples of **Jesse Windows** from this period. The vine now covered up to seven lights, ignoring the mullions. The ovals were filled up with diaper pattern, different in colour to the vine's background. The vine was now more true to life. There are examples at Madley (Herefordshire), Wells Cathedral, and Selby Abbey.

Tracery Lights were filled with foliage patterns, grotesque beasts, human heads with their name, saints, or even picture subjects. The emblems of the four Evangelists, and shields were also used. Near the end of the century more diaper patterns and yellow stain appear as backgrounds in traceries. In both the fourteenth century and the fifteenth century angels other than those in the Nine Orders are shown in two ways. In one they wear white robes, and in the other their bodies are covered with gold feathers—a treatment also seen in performances of Miracle Plays. It was at this stage, too, that the process of abrading was first used on flash glass. Poses and facial expressions tended to become less reserved, and more realistic.

The Fifteenth Century, Late Gothic, or Perpendicular Period

By now the wealthy middle classes could afford to put up vast amounts of stained glass, and more glass has survived than from previous centuries. The leads stopped playing such an important part in the design, and were regarded as a nuisance rather than the strength that they are. Generally, drawing started to take precedence over the skills of glazing —except when small pieces of pot-metal were laboriously let into shields, or else into the hems of clothes to represent jewels. But the drawing could be marvellous—detailed, subtle, and crisp.

Quarry Windows were an extension of the grisaille windows, and great favourites at this time. The quarries were diamond-shaped, and individually decorated with small stained emblems. These included flowers, insects, leaves, birds, and heraldic devices or marks. They were varied, and often beautifully drawn. All-over leaf patterns were abandoned. Figures, shields, roundels, and strap borders were placed on quarry backgrounds as before.

Figure and Canopy Windows are the windows most often found in the fifteenth century. The movement of the S pose disappeared from the figures, which were large. Faces are finely drawn, and stipple, smear, and line are used to suggest shadow and form. Highlights are obtained by scratching through the smear. Hair was usually stained yellow, but haloes were sometimes still leaded separately. Differences from fourteenth century canopy windows have already been mentioned. The thing that strikes the viewer most is that eventually the pinnacles of the canopies make windows look like grottoes festooned with icicles. The simplicity of earlier periods is preferable.

Subject Windows were extremely popular, and drew upon many of the subjects discussed earlier. The subjects were arranged in rows across the lights, each one having its own canopy. Sometimes descriptions, or articles from the Creed were written in black-letter script between the rows. The pictures were quite simple for the period. In the second half of the century two changes took place. One was that subject windows spread over two or three lights—as in the subject of the Crucifixion. The other was that, due to continental influence, the canopy was often left out, so that figures or subjects could occupy the whole of the light.

The demand for **Jesse Windows** declined, and few fifteenth century examples remain. The one at Margaretting (Essex) is the best. The figures in the ovals are in pairs.

Tracery Lights were very important in the fifteenth century. The same subjects are found, except that more angels occur. They sometimes held shields. Heraldry, indeed, was a flourishing subject for stained glass. This, too, is the century of the donor in stained glass. Whole families are shown, kneeling in prayer, and arranged in rows behind each other. If high in rank, they may be shown at a desk, reading from a book.

The Sixteenth Century, or Renaissance Period

At the end of the last period the white glass had acquired a delicate, silvery quality. But simplicity, strength, and brilliance were gradually being lost from stained glass, and in the sixteenth century they disappeared. This was largely due to the influence of the continental Renaissance. The art of the Renaissance was man-orientated, not god-orientated, and it therefore clashed with the art of stained glass in a very fundamental way. Renaissance artists were interested in the human body, and in its concrete surroundings. Anatomy was

47

studied, and perspective mastered. These preoccupations made themselves felt in stained glass. While the types of window stayed the same, the treatment was very different.

Figures were more realistic, and were set in solid-looking landscapes, complete with buildings, skies, trees, and birds. Or else they were surrounded by interiors filled with their belongings and furniture. A clutter of objects seems to press in on the figures: there is pride in their possession, and virtuosity in their presentation. The result is a materialistic air which is out of keeping with stained glass. Shading is produced by heavy stippling—a cruder and more mechanical texture than that produced by line drawing. Canopies are heavier and clumsier. Architecture is an uneasy mixture of Gothic and Classical. Features such as fluted columns, architraves and scroll-work, cupids and garlands tend to make the effect insipid. Leadwork had lost most of its importance as an element of design.

In other words, stained glass was imitating contemporary painting, and must be judged by similar standards. It was in heraldic work alone that the essential qualities of the craft were maintained. Shields were often complicated, and contained a large number of "quarterings". Since religious glass was banned after the Reformation, heraldic glass was in great demand. Some religious glass, however, was still made for private worship.

About the middle of the sixteenth century it was discovered that coloured glass paints or "enamels" could be made from powdered coloured glass mixed with a medium. When such painting was fired it fused with the surface of the glass. Not only did this tend to flake, but because it made lead unnecessary it helped to bring about the final deterioration of stained glass in the seventeenth and eighteenth centuries.

The Seventeenth Century Period

Much glass of this period is given a date. At first the new enamel paints were used to supplement more traditional techniques. This is the case with the heraldic panels made by Dininckhoff. In common with some painted heraldic glass of a later date, there is drawing of a very high standard here. The tendency in heraldic glass, however, was to great elaboration and realism of detail, and in the work of Henry Gyles, for example, this finally becomes oppressive.

In 1636 Louis XIII invaded Lorraine, and as an act of retribution laid waste much of the duchy, including the glassworks. Pot-metal became unobtainable, and enamel paints came into their own. For a period white glass was simply cut into rectangles, and the leads became a grille. Oxford is the best place to study windows of this kind. The most arresting are by Bernard and Abraham Van Linge, who left England when Civil War broke out. Wadham, Lincoln, Balliol, Christ Church, and University Colleges, as well as Lydiard Tregoze Church, Wiltshire, all have examples. They are arresting, but not necessarily good. They are crowded with too much detail, and figures are painted in "realistic" flesh tints. They are neither stained glass, nor paintings. The impression is of great ability misdirected.

There are attractive portraits on glass by Richard Greenbury in several Oxford colleges. The best known are of Charles I and his Queen, at Magdalen College. Another famous glass painter of the day was Baptista Sutton, an Englishman. There are windows by him in the Chapel of the Holy Trinity, Guildford. Other interesting examples by various people are to be found at: the Chapel of Trinity Hospital, Greenwich; Peterhouse College Chapel, Cambridge; Compton (Surrey); Sellack and Abbey Dore (Herefordshire); and Low Ham (Som.).

Much glass of the period belongs to the history of antique painted domestic glass, rather than to the history of stained glass. Quarries and roundels were painted with a great variety of charming pictures. Stained glass sundials were common. A fly was painted on many of them—a pictorial pun on the motto *Dum spectas fugio*, "Even as you watch I am flying". Gyles, who has already been mentioned, charged £1 for a sundial.

The Eighteenth Century Period

Whereas stained glass in the seventeenth century had been mostly heraldic in character the advent of the eighteenth century saw a renewed demand for figurative windows. Already in 1696 William Price the Elder had painted a Nativity window for Christ Church, Oxford. He went on to complete the vast east window of Merton College chapel, Oxford, in 1702 (this was removed in the 1930s but part of it is now on exhibition at the Stained Glass Museum, Ely Cathedral). From 1719 to 1722 his younger brother, Joshua Price, executed Francisco Slater's designs for a fine series of windows now placed in Great Witley Church, Worcestershire. About 1732 John Rowell of High Wycombe painted idiosyncratic windows which have survived at the chapel of The Vyne, Hampshire, and at Apethorpe, Northamptonshire.

Throughout the eighteenth century stained glass was thought of in terms of a translucent oil painting. It was made of rectangular panels of glass of a regular size, and only rarely was lead used to follow the outlines of the drawing. By the middle of the century William Peckitt of York (1731–95) was the leading figure in stained glass. He was successful in producing a type of 'flashed' ruby glass in the 1780s but coloured glass was generally little used by Georgian glass painters, colour mostly being achieved by using enamel paints. There is a stunning Peckitt Last Supper window at Audley End, Essex, made in 1771 from designs by Biagio Rebecca, and his work can also be seen at St Martin-cum-Gregory, York, and in the library of Trinity College, Cambridge.

In the latter part of the century the most accomplished stained glass artists were Francis Eginton–a protege of Boulton and Watt in Birmingham and very much a craftsman of the industrial revolution–and James Pearson, who came to London from Dublin. The Conversion of St Paul east window of St Paul's, Birmingham (1789), designed by the American painter Sir Benjamin West, is Eginton's *chef d'oeuvre*: dark and dramatic, it shows Eginton striving for a deliberately theatrical effect. Equally theatrical, but this time light and delicate in tone, is his east window of St Alkmund's, Shrewsbury, of 1795, the design of which was lifted from Guido Reni's *Assumption of the Virgin*. The largest and boldest surviving window by James Pearson is his Moses and the Brazen Serpent, adapted from a painting by J. H. Mortimer, which graces the upper east window of Salisbury Cathedral. It will be clear how pictorial the approach of these artists was from the names of the painters listed above whose designs were used for windows. The most renowned example of this sort of collaboration was the ante-chapel window of New College, Oxford, made by Thomas Jervais in 1777–83. The designs were provided by Sir Joshua Reynolds, the leading Academician of the day, and the resulting window has often been cited as representing the depths to which stained glass fell in the eighteenth century. It is certainly the antithesis of great medieval stained glass, but seen from an unprejudiced viewpoint there is much to commend in this dramatic and intriguing window.

The Nineteenth Century Period

The rapid growth in population in the nineteenth century, together with the effects of the Anglo-Catholic revival of worship and the Gothic revival in architecture, resulted in a vast increase in the demand for new stained glass. An unprecedented volume of windows was made in England for buildings both here and abroad, and stained glass became a booming industry. Considering the quantity of work for which the larger studios were responsible the surprise is that standards remained as high as they did, though later in the century there was a tendency for their approach to become stereotyped and mechanical.

The romantic manner of the Georgian glass painters was steadily supplanted by a more archaeologically accurate approach to the subject. Thomas Willement was an important pioneer of medievalising stained glass, Charles Winston wrote extensively and practically on the subject and was responsible for great improvements in the quality of glass available, and Pugin was almost as influential in the field of stained glass as he was in architecture. Medieval style revivals became the order of the day until 1861, when William Morris founded his famous decorative arts firm together with his friends Rossetti, Madox Brown and Burne-Jones. Typically excellent series by Morris and Co, both dating from the 1870s, can be seen at Oxford Cathedral and Jesus College chapel, Cambridge, and of their later work the windows of Birmingham Cathedral are outstanding.

One outcome of the recent reassessment of the Victorian period is that artists other than those from the immediate Pre-Raphaelite circle are being given their due. Of the earlier men Thomas Willement, who was stained glass artist to Queen Victoria, made an extensive series for St George's Chapel, Windsor, and amongst many fine windows designed by Pugin the great west window of Ushaw College chapel, Durham, is remarkably refined and elegant. Contemporaries of Morris who followed a slightly more traditional, though still inventive, path were Clayton and Bell (who made the stunning Last Judgement window at Hanley Castle church, Worcestershire, in 1860), Heaton, Butler and Bayne (Te Deum window, All Saints, Clapham Park, London, 1862) and Lavers and Barraud (scenes from Tennyson's *Idylls of the King*, Northampton Town Hall, 1862). C. E. Kempe and Burlison and Grylls became the leading protagonists of the later Gothic revival in stained glass: West Kirby, Merseyside, has a complete set of Kempe windows and Bodley's churches at Pendlebury, Greater Manchester, and Hoar Cross, Staffordshire, have fine examples of the work of Burlison and Grylls. Of the artists originally influenced by the Pre-Raphaelites the most original was Henry Holiday: Mortlake church has a beautiful Annunciation from his early period and Southwark Cathedral's Creation window is one of his best late works.

Towards the end of the nineteenth century there was a growing reaction against the factory-like streamlining of production methods which many Victorian firms had adopted to cope with the great demand for stained glass. A new generation of Arts and Crafts Movement workers, emerging from about 1890, demanded that the designer of a window should be responsible for all stages of its execution. Led by Christopher Whall and armed with a new variety of thick and coarsely textured glass, they produced stained glass of a revived spirit and freshness. Good examples by Whall himself are at Burford, Oxfordshire, and Ashbourne, Derbyshire. By the turn of the century English stained glass held a leading position in the world.

The Twentieth Century Period

It is perhaps too early yet to make judgements about twentieth-century stained glass. In general it is true to say that English stained glass has remained more traditional in style than much other European work, and countries such as Germany have tended to lead the field, certainly in abstract stained glass. By the outbreak of the First World War the Arts and Crafts Movement was losing its impetus. Those who had continued with basically Gothic styles such as Sir Ninian Comper, F. C. Eden and the brothers Christopher and Geoffrey Webb, continued to be prolific in the inter-war years and their glass was always refined, if sometimes rather lack-lustre. Much less compromising was the approach of two Irish ladies, Wilhelmina Geddes and Evie Hone. Evie Hone made powerful–almost overpowering–east windows for Eton College chapel and St Michael's, Highgate, London, in the 1950s and her reputation has overshadowed that of Miss Geddes, whose early work, such as the Crucifixion east window (1922) of St Luke, Wallsend-on-Tyne, bears comparison with anything of its time.

In the period since 1945 some of the most popular stained glass artists have worked in very personal figurative styles, such as Ervin Bossanyi (Canterbury Cathedral, Tate Gallery) and Hugh Easton (Holy Trinity, Coventry). Also figurative were the first windows designed by John Piper, made for Oundle School chapel, Northamptonshire, in 1955. Executed in collaboration with Patrick Reyntiens, these were a milestone in modern English stained glass. Still probably the best known example designed by Piper is the baptistry window of the new Coventry Cathedral (1962). The nave windows here were made by a team from the Royal College of Art, Lawrence Lee, Keith New and Geoffrey Clarke, all of whom have done interesting work elsewhere. The 1970s saw a welcome resurgence of interest in stained glass in England and there are signs that this is beginning to be reflected in the work of a younger generation of artists. The most precocious of these is Brian Clarke (born 1953), who has designed cool and thoughtful windows for St Gabriel's, Blackburn, Queen's Medical Centre, Nottingham, and Longridge church, Lancashire. For stained glass to have a healthy future which can reflect its glorious past it is essential that more patronage is forthcoming from the secular field, now that ecclesiastical commissions are dwindling. In the USA the 'autonomous' or free-standing panel has become a popular mode of expression in stained glass, and these are sold in galleries in the same way as paintings. However only stained glass conceived as an integral element in the architecture of the future will ensure the continuing development of this ancient but still promising medium.

PLACES CONTAINING INTERESTING STAINED GLASS

The numbers in this list refer to centuries. For example, at Bristol Cathedral there is interesting glass of the fourteenth, fifteenth, nineteenth and twentieth centuries.

AVON. Bristol Cathedral 14, 15, 19, 20. Brockley 19. Winscombe 15, 16, 19.

BEDFORDSHIRE. Cockayne Hatley 14, 15, 18. Edworth 14. Northill 17.

BERKSHIRE. Aldermaston 13. Bradfield College 19. Bucklebury 20. Eton College 20. Ockwells Manor 15. Stratfield Mortimer: St John 15, 19. Windsor: St George 19.

BUCKINGHAMSHIRE. Bradenham 16,18. Chetwode 13, 14. Drayton Beauchamp 15. Hillesden 16. Monks Risborough 15. Stoke Poges 17, 19. Turville 16, 18.

CAMBRIDGESHIRE. Brinkley 14. Buckden 15. Cambridge: Christ's College 15, 16; King's College 16; Peterhouse 17, 19; Trinity College 18, 19. Diddington 15, 16, 17. Ely: Cathedral 14, 19; Stained Glass Museum 14, 15, 17, 18, 19, 20. Haslingfield 14. Leverington 15. Meldreth 14. Sawtry 15, 16. Trumpington 13. Wistow 15.

CHESHIRE. Disley 16. Grappenhall 16. Shotwick 14.

CORNWALL. St Kew 15. St Neot 15, 16. St Winnow 15, 16. Truro Cathedral 19.

CUMBRIA. Bowness 15. Cartmel Fell 15. Greystoke 15. Keswick 19, 20. Tolson Hall 17. Windermere: St John Evangelist 20.

DERBYSHIRE. Ashbourne 13, 14, 15, 19, 20. Dalbury 14. Darley Dale 19. Dronfield 14. Morley 15. Norbury 14, 15. Staveley 14, 17, 20. Wilne 17.

DEVON. Ashton 15. Bampton 15. Bere Ferrers 14. Broadwood Kelly 16. Doddiscombsleigh 15, 16. Exeter Cathedral 14, 20. Ottery St Mary 19.

DORSET. Abbotsbury 14, 18. Bradford Peverell 15. Melbury Bubb 15. Sherborne Abbey 19.

DURHAM. Darlington: St Cuthbert 19. Durham Cathedral 15, 19. Lanchester 13.

EAST SUSSEX. Bexhill: St Peter 15. Brighton: St Michael 19. Ovingdean 19. Rottingdean 19. Ticehurst 14. Winchelsea 14, 20.

ESSEX. Audley End 18; College of St Mark 15. Clavering 15. Great Burstead 15. Harlow 14, 18, 19. Heybridge 13. Margaretting 15. Messing 17. Rivenhall 12, 13. Stapleford Abbots 14. Thaxted 14, 15. Waltham Abbey 19. White Notley 13.

GLOUCESTERSHIRE. Arlingham 14. Bagendon 15, 20. Bledington 15. Buckland 15. Cirencester 15. Coln Rogers 15. Deerhurst 14. Fairford 16.

Gloucester Cathedral 14, 19, 20. North Cerney: All Saints 15. Temple Guiting 15. Tewkesbury Abbey 14.

GREATER LONDON. Central London: All Saints, Margaret Street 19; St George, Hanover Square 16; St Margaret, Westminster 16, 19, 20; Victoria and Albert Museum — all periods; Westminster Abbey 13, 15, 18, 19, 20. Clapham Park: All Saints 19. Greenwich: Trinity Hospital 16. West Wickham 16. Wimbledon: St Mary 14, 17, 20.

GREATER MANCHESTER. Ashton-under-Lyne 15, 16. Middleton 16.

HAMPSHIRE. Basingstoke: St Michael 16. Bramley 14, 16. East Tytherley 13. Grateley 13. Headley 13. Herriard 14. Mottisfont 15. Sherborne St John: chapel of The Vyne 16; tomb chamber 18. Winchester: Cathedral 15, 16, 19; College chapel 14, 19; St Cross Hospital 15, 19.

HEREFORD AND WORCESTER. Abbey Dore 15, 16, 17. Bredon 14. Brinsop 14, 20. Credenhill 14. Eaton Bishop 14. Fladbury 14, 19. Great Malvern Priory 15, 19. Great Witley 18. Hereford Cathedral 14, 19. Holt 15. Kempsey 14. Ledbury 13, 16, 19. Little Malvern 15. Madley 13, 14. Mamble 14. Oddingley 16. Ross 15. Sellack 15, 16. Warndon 14, 15. Weobley 15. Worcester Cathedral 19.

HERTFORDSHIRE. Barkway 14, 15, 16. Barley 14, 15, 16. King's Walden 19. St Paul's Walden 14, 20. South Mimms 16. Waterford 19.

HUMBERSIDE. Barton|upon| Humber 14. Beverley Minster 13, 14, 15, 19. Harpham 18. Hotham 20. Redbourne 19.

KENT. Boughton Aluph 14. Brabourne 12, 15. Canterbury Cathedral 12, 13, 15, 20. Chartham 15. Chilham 15. Doddington 13. Fawkham 14. Nackington 13. Nettlestead 15. Selling 14. Tonbridge School 20. Upper Hardres 13, 14. Westwell 13, 14. Wormshill 15.

LANCASHIRE. Longridge 20.

LEICESTERSHIRE. Appleby 14. Ayston 15. Leicester Museum 15. North Luffenham 14. Thornton 14. Twycross 12, 13. Whitwell 14. Withcote 16.

LINCOLNSHIRE. Carlton Scroop 14. Heydour 14. Lincoln Cathedral 12, 13, 14, 18, 19. Long Sutton 14. Raithby-by-Louth 19. Stamford: Browne's Hospital 15; St George 15; St Martin 15, 19. Stragglethorpe 13. Tattershall 15. Wrangle 14.

MERSEYSIDE. Liverpool Cathedral 20. West Kirby 19.

NORFOLK. Bawburgh 15. East Harling 15. Elsing 14. Ketteringham 15. Langley 16. Martham 15. Mulbarton 15. North Elmham 14. North Tuddenham 15. Norwich: Cathedral 16, 19; St John Baptist (RC) 19; St Peter Hungate Museum 15, 16; St Peter Mancroft 15, 20. Saxlingham Nethergate 13, 14, 15. Shelton 15, 16. South Acre 13. Stratton Strawless 15. Thurton 15, 16, 17, 18.

NORTHAMPTONSHIRE. Aldwincle 14. Hollowell 19. Lowick 14. Middleton Cheney 19. Rushden 15. Stanford-on-Avon 14, 15, 16. Watford 19.

NORTHUMBERLAND. Bothal 14. Morpeth: St Mary 14.

NORTH YORKSHIRE. Coxwold 15, 18. Denton-in-Wharfedale 18. Gilling Castle 16. Selby Abbey 14, 19. York: All Saints 15; Holy Trinity, Goodramgate 15; Minster 13, 14, 15, 16, 17, 18, 19, 20; St Denys, Walmgate 14, 15; St Helen 14, 15; St Martin 15; St Michael, Spurriergate 15, 16.

NOTTINGHAMSHIRE. Hawton 14. Holme-by-Newark 15. Newark 14, 15, 19. Southwell Minster 14, 16, 17, 19.

OXFORDSHIRE. Bloxham 19. Childrey 15. Chinnor 14. Dorchester 13, 14. Harpsden 15. Horspath 13, 14, 15, 16. Kidlington 13. Marsh Baldon 14, 15. Oxford: All Souls College 15; Balliol College 16, 17; Brasenose College 18; Cathedral 14, 17, 19; Exeter College 19; Lincoln College 17; Magdalen College 17, 19; Merton College 13, 15, 16; New College 14, 18; Queen's College 16, 17, 18; Trinity College 14, 15, 16, 17, 19; University College 17, 19. South Newington 14. Stanford-in-the-Vale 14. Stanton Harcourt 13, 15. Stanton St John 13, 14. Yarnton 15, 16, 17.

SALOP. Atcham 15. Donington 14. Ludlow 14, 15, 19. Prees 19. Shrewsbury: St Mary 14, 15, 16, 17, 19. Upton Magna 19.

SOMERSET. Axbridge Town Hall 15. Compton Bishop 14. Langport 15. Low Ham 17. Wells Cathedral 14, 15, 19, 20.

STAFFORDSHIRE. Amington 19. Hamstall Ridware 14, 19. Leigh 14, 19. Lichfield Cathedral 16, 19. Okeover 14, 19. Trysull 14, 19.

SUFFOLK. Barton Mills 14. Brandeston 16. Bury St Edmunds Cathedral 16, 19. Combs 15. Gipping 15. Hengrave Hall 16. Hessett 15, 16. Ipswich: St Matthew 19. Long Melford 15. Thorndon 14, 15.

SURREY. Ashtead 16. Buckland 14. Compton 13, 15. Guildford: Abbot's Hospital 15. Laleham 20. Sutton Place 16, 17, 19. West Horsley 13.

TYNE AND WEAR. Newcastle upon Tyne: St John Baptist 15. Wallsend: St Luke 20.

WARWICKSHIRE. Arley 14. Cherington 14, 15, 16, 17, 18. Coughton 16. Mancetter 14. Merevale 14, 15. Warwick: St Mary 15.

WEST MIDLANDS. Aston 18. Birmingham: Cathedral 19; St Paul 18. Coventry: Cathedral 15, 20; St Mary's Hall 15, 20. Dudley: St Thomas 19. Wightwick Manor 19.

WEST SUSSEX. Arundel: St Philip Neri 19. Chichester Cathedral 19, 20.

WEST YORKSHIRE. Adel 17. Almondbury 15. Ilkley 19, 20. Rothwell 18, 19. Thornhill 15, 18.

WILTSHIRE. Cricklade: St Sampson 19, 20. Crudwell 15. Edington 15. Lydiard Tregoze 17. Salisbury Cathedral 13, 14, 17, 18, 19, 20. Stourhead 15. Wilton 12, 13, 14, 15, 16, 17.

The Stained Glass Museum, North Triforium, Ely Cathedral

The Stained Glass Museum was established in 1973 to act as a repository and display space for stained glass from redundant churches and other buildings. It is open to the public daily from the end of March to the end of October. Visits in the winter months are normally by appointment only.

The museum has on display stained glass of all periods ranging from the early fourteenth century to a selection of brand-new work, and models showing how stained glass is manufactured. The variety of glass shown is wide: there are several examples dating from the fourteenth century – a two-light 'Annunciation' from Hadzor church, Worcestershire, being outstanding, panels by Burne-Jones and Henry Holiday, and special displays of High Victorian stained glass, Scottish stained glass and Georgian stained glass – all areas of study which have previously been neglected.

FURTHER READING

Baker, John. *English Stained Glass of the Medieval Period.* Thames and Hudson, 1978.

Clarke, Brian (editor). *Architectural Stained Glass.* John Murray, 1979.

Harrison, Martin. *Victorian Stained Glass.* Barrie and Jenkins, 1980.

Lee, Lawrence. *The Appreciation of Stained Glass.* Oxford University Press, 1977.

Reyntiens, Patrick. *Technique of Stained Glass.* Batsford, 1977.